301 Fascinating Facts: Cars, Trucks and Trains Edition

M.K. Publishing House

Copyright © [2024] by [M.K. Publishing House]

All rights reserved.

No portion of this book may be reproduced in any form without written permission from the publisher or author, except as permitted by U.S. copyright law.

Contents

1. Epic Engines — 1
2. Record-Breaking Rides — 12
3. Famous Cars and Trucks in Movies and TV — 23
4. From Horsepower to Electric Power — 34
5. Mega Machines — 45
6. Wild Wheels — 56
7. Train Routes Around the World — 67
8. Off-Road Adventure Machines — 78
9. How Traffic Works — 89
10. Dream Cars of the Future — 100

Contents

Chapter One

Epic Engines

How Cars, Trucks, and Trains Run Explore the engines that power different vehicles, from small car engines to powerful train locomotives.

1. Did you know that a car engine works kind of like a birthday cake mixer? Just like a mixer uses spinning blades to blend ingredients, your car's engine has special parts called pistons that move up and down super fast to mix fuel and air together. When this mixture explodes (in tiny, controlled bursts), it creates the power that makes your car zoom down the road!

2. Train engines are like the superheroes of the engine world! They're so powerful that just one modern

train engine can pull as much weight as 170 big trucks combined. Imagine having the strength to pull 2,000 elephants at once – that's how strong a train engine is! These mighty machines help move everything from food to furniture across entire countries.

3. The first car engines were pretty silly compared to today's versions. They were so weak that people had to get out and push their cars up hills! These old engines made about 12 horsepower – that's like having just 12 horses pulling your car. Today's regular cars have around 200 horsepower, which is why they zoom up hills without breaking a sweat.

4. Here's something crazy about truck engines: they can run non-stop for days! Long-haul trucks are built with special heavy-duty engines that can keep going for millions of miles. That's like driving around the Earth 40 times! These engines are built extra tough and have special oil systems that keep them running smoothly,

just like how drinking water keeps you going during sports.

5. Ever wondered why engines make that vrooming sound? It's because tiny explosions are happening inside! When fuel and air mix together and explode, it makes a pop sound. In a car engine, this happens thousands of times every minute. It's like having thousands of tiny firecrackers going off super fast – that's what creates that familiar engine roar!

6. Race car engines are like the cheetahs of the engine world – they're built for speed, not comfort! These special engines can spin up to 18,000 times per minute. That's so fast that if you tried to count that high, it would take you hours! Regular car engines only spin about 3,000 times per minute when you're driving on the highway.

7. Electric car engines are like ninja warriors – they're super powerful but totally silent! Unlike regular cars

that go "vroom," electric engines make almost no noise at all. They're also much simpler than gas engines, with fewer moving parts. It's like comparing a complicated Lego set with hundreds of pieces to one with just a few pieces.

8. Did you know that big truck engines have their own mini-computers? These smart computers help the engine use just the right amount of fuel, kind of like how your brain tells you when to eat more or less food. They can even tell the driver when something's wrong, like a doctor checking if you're feeling sick!

9. Train engines are so strong that they need special wheels to handle all their power! The wheels are made with super-hard steel and are connected to the engine through something called a "drivetrain." It's like having the strongest bicycle chain ever – but way, way bigger and tougher!

10. Car engines have something called spark plugs, which are like tiny lightning makers! These special plugs create small electric sparks that help ignite the fuel in your engine. Without spark plugs, your car would be like a birthday cake without candles – it just wouldn't work! Each spark is as hot as a bolt of lightning.

11. Some big trucks have engines that are as large as your bedroom! These massive engines can be six feet tall and weigh as much as five cars put together. Inside these giants, pistons the size of beach balls move up and down to create power. It's like having a whole gymnasium full of machinery working together!

12. Steam train engines were like giant tea kettles on wheels! They needed someone called a fireman to keep shoving coal into a big fire, which heated water to make steam. The steam pushed huge pistons that turned the wheels. It's like using hot steam from a kettle to spin a pinwheel, but much, much bigger!

13. Modern car engines are like super-smart robots! They have special sensors that check everything happening inside the engine thousands of times per second. That's faster than you can blink! These sensors help the engine run smoothly and use less fuel, kind of like having a tiny scientist monitoring everything.

14. Hybrid cars are extra special because they have two different types of engines working together – like best friends! One engine uses gasoline (like a regular car), and the other is electric (like a giant battery-powered toy). They take turns doing the work, which helps save fuel and keeps the air cleaner.

15. Engine oil is like a superhero juice for engines! Without it, all the metal parts inside would get super hot and stick together – ouch! The oil helps everything slide smoothly, just like how soap helps you wash your hands. Every engine needs regular oil changes to stay healthy, just like how you need to drink water every day.

16. Some train engines are so powerful they need special cooling systems bigger than your school bus! These systems use huge fans and gallons of coolant to keep the engine from getting too hot. It's like having a swimming pool-sized water bottle to keep the engine cool while it works hard pulling heavy train cars.

17. Engine air filters are like face masks for engines! They stop dirt and dust from getting inside and causing trouble, just like how a mask stops germs. Without an air filter, an engine would get sick and stop working properly. That's why mechanics check and change them regularly, like changing the filter in a fish tank.

18. Did you know that engines have something called cylinders? These are like secret rooms where the power is made! Most car engines have four, six, or eight cylinders, but some fancy sports cars have twelve or more. It's like having a bunch of mini rocket launchers all working together to make your car move.

19. Truck engines have something amazing called a turbocharger – it's like a tiny tornado maker! This special part spins super fast and pushes extra air into the engine, giving it more power. It's similar to how blowing on a pinwheel makes it spin faster, but the turbocharger spins about 100,000 times per minute!

20. Engine temperature gauges are like thermometers for your car! They tell you if the engine is too hot or too cold, just like how a thermometer tells if you have a fever. If an engine gets too hot, it can get damaged – that's why cars have warning lights to let you know when something's wrong.

21. Some modern engines can actually turn themselves off when you stop at a red light! This clever trick helps save fuel and keeps the air cleaner. When you press the gas pedal, the engine starts up again faster than you can say "green light!" It's like having a engine that takes quick power naps.

22. Engine blocks are like the skeleton of an engine – they hold everything together! These huge pieces of metal are made by pouring super-hot liquid metal into special molds. Once the metal cools down, it becomes super strong. It's like making jello, but with metal that can withstand thousands of tiny explosions!

23. Train engines have special "governors" that control their speed, kind of like having a strict teacher making sure you don't run in the hallway! These governors make sure the engine doesn't go too fast and break itself. They're like a built-in speed limit sign that the train has to follow.

24. Some truck engines have something called a "jake brake" that helps them slow down without using regular brakes! It's like having a magic power that turns the engine into a brake. When truck drivers use it, it makes a loud "brrrraaaap" sound that you might have heard on the highway!

25. Racing engines have special parts made from super-light materials like titanium! This metal is as strong as steel but much lighter, which helps the cars go faster. It's like building a bicycle out of feathers that are as strong as rocks – pretty amazing, right? These parts cost more than a whole regular car!

26. Electric train engines are like giant battery-powered toys! They get their power from electric lines above the track or a third rail running alongside. The electricity flows through the engine like water through a hose, making powerful motors turn the wheels. It's much cleaner and quieter than old steam engines.

27. Some car engines can power your house during a blackout! These special hybrid cars have engines that can be used as generators, providing electricity to keep your lights on and your fridge running. It's like having a backup power plant sitting in your driveway – how cool is that?

28. Modern engines have something called direct injection, which is like having a super-precise squirt gun for fuel! It shoots tiny amounts of fuel exactly where it needs to go, at exactly the right time. This helps the engine use less fuel and run better, like a chef using exactly the right amount of ingredients.

29. Big ship engines are the giants of the engine world! Some are as tall as a three-story building and as long as a whole football field. These monsters can push ships that are bigger than several football fields through rough ocean waves. They're so big that engineers can actually walk inside them for maintenance!

30. Did you know that some engines can run on french fry oil? It's true! Some diesel engines can be modified to run on used cooking oil from restaurants. Instead of the smell of exhaust, these cars leave behind the smell of french fries as they drive by. It's like recycling your lunch to power your car!

Chapter Two

Record-Breaking Rides

Fastest, Biggest, and Longest Vehicles Fascinating facts on the fastest cars, biggest trucks, and longest trains in history.

1. Would you believe that the fastest car in the world can drive faster than an airplane taking off? The Bugatti Chiron Super Sport 300+ zoomed to an incredible speed of 304.77 miles per hour! That's like traveling the length of three football fields in just one second. The car looks like a rocket on wheels and costs more than 3 million dollars!

2. Have you heard of the BelAZ 75710? It's the biggest dump truck in the entire world! This monster truck is as tall as a three-story building and weighs as much as 100 elephants. Its tires are bigger than your bedroom – each one is 13 feet tall! You need a special ladder just to climb up to the driver's seat.

3. Imagine a train so long it takes 10 minutes to pass by! The longest train ever was in Australia, and it had 682 train cars attached to it. If you laid this train out straight, it would be 4.57 miles long! That's the same as 80 football fields put together. It needed eight huge engines just to pull everything.

4. The most expensive car ever sold was a super rare 1955 Mercedes-Benz that cost $142 million! That's enough money to buy a mansion in every state. Only two of these special cars were ever made, and they have cool doors that open up like wings. It's like having a transformer in your garage!

5. Did you know there's a bus that's longer than three school buses combined? The AutoTram Extra Grand from Germany is 98 feet long and can carry 256 people at once. That's like moving an entire elementary school on one bus! It bends in the middle like a caterpillar to help it turn corners.

6. The biggest airplane ever built had wings longer than a football field! The Antonov An-225 could carry 14 fully loaded trucks in its belly. This giant of the sky was so heavy that it needed 32 wheels to land safely. Sadly, this amazing plane was destroyed in 2022, but it broke many records during its life.

7. Want to hear something crazy? There's a truck called Thor 24 that has as much power as 40 regular cars combined! This super-truck has 24 cylinders and 12 superchargers (that's like having 12 jet engines helping the truck go faster). It looks like something from a superhero movie with chrome pipes everywhere!

8. Japan has a train that doesn't even touch the tracks – it floats using giant magnets! The L0 Series Maglev is the fastest train ever, reaching speeds of 374 miles per hour. That's twice as fast as a race car! If this train ran between New York and Philadelphia, you could make the trip in just 15 minutes.

9. The biggest vehicle ever made doesn't go on roads – it carries rockets! NASA's Crawler-Transporter is as big as a baseball field and moves super slowly, about as fast as a turtle walks. Each of its giant tracks has 57 shoes, and each shoe weighs as much as your family car!

10. Ever seen a ship so big it could hold 126 swimming pools full of oil? The Seawise Giant was the largest ship ever built – longer than the Empire State Building is tall! If you wanted to walk from one end to the other, it would take about 10 minutes. That's like walking five blocks just to get across one ship!

11. Here's something wild about those super-fast Bugatti cars – each tire costs more than a fancy swimming pool! At $42,000 per tire, that's more than many people spend on their whole car. And get this: they need to be changed every 2,500 miles because going so fast wears them out really quickly!

12. The world's fastest electric car is the Rimac Nevera, which can go from standing still to 60 miles per hour in less than two seconds! That's faster than you can say "supercalifragilisticexpialidocious." It's like having four Formula 1 race cars worth of power in one vehicle!

13. Want to know about the strongest motorcycle ever? The Dodge Tomahawk has an engine from a car and can go over 300 miles per hour! It has four wheels instead of two, making it look like something from the future. Only nine were ever made, and each one cost $555,000 – that's like buying 25 regular motorcycles!

14. The longest limousine ever made was as long as three tennis courts! It had 26 wheels and included a swimming pool, a king-sized bed, and even a helicopter landing pad on the back. This crazy car needed two drivers to operate it – one in the front and one in the back to help it turn corners!

15. Meet the Monster Jam truck Bigfoot #5 – it has tires taller than your house! These tires came from military vehicles and are 10 feet tall. When Bigfoot #5 drives over regular cars, it makes them look like toy cars. The driver needs to climb up a very tall ladder just to get into the cab!

16. Did you know there's a train that runs through a building? The Chongqing Rail Transit in China goes right through the middle of a 19-story apartment building! Imagine having a train pass through your building every few minutes. Don't worry – special sound-proofing keeps it super quiet for the residents.

17. The world's smallest production car is the Peel P50, and it's smaller than some office desks! It only has three wheels and one door, and it's so light that a strong person can pick it up and move it around. You could park three of them in a regular parking space!

18. Ever heard of an amphibious vehicle? The LARC-LX is like a boat and truck combined! It's as tall as a four-story building and can drive on land or float in water. The military uses these giant machines to move heavy equipment from ships to shore, like a duck that can carry tanks!

19. The fastest boat ever made is the Spirit of Australia, which zoomed across the water at 317 miles per hour! That's faster than many airplanes. The boat used a jet engine from an airplane to reach these incredible speeds, and it created a rooster tail of water higher than a five-story building!

20. Ready for something really cool? The biggest helicopter ever built can lift as much weight as 14 elephants! The Mil Mi-26 is like a flying house and can even carry other helicopters inside it. Its rotor blades are so long that they could stretch across a basketball court!

21. The heaviest tank ever built was the German Panzer VIII Maus from World War II. It weighed as much as 75 regular cars put together! The tank was so heavy that it could barely move through mud, and most bridges couldn't support its weight. Only two were ever built!

22. Here's a wild fact: The biggest RV in the world costs more than most mansions! The eleMMent Palazzo Superior looks like a spaceship on wheels and has a pop-out deck on top. Inside, it's fancier than a five-star hotel, with marble floors and a master bedroom bigger than most living rooms!

23. The fastest street-legal bicycle reached speeds of 89 miles per hour! That's faster than cars on the highway. It

uses a special aerodynamic shell that makes it look like a bullet, and the rider has to lay down flat to go super fast. Regular bikes only go about 15 miles per hour!

24. Did you know there's a car that can transform into a plane in just three minutes? The AirCar can drive on roads like a normal car, but when it reaches an airport, its wings fold out and it takes to the sky! It's like having your own private transformer that can fly you over traffic jams.

25. The biggest fire truck in the world is the Hawaiian Airport Crash Tender. It can spray water higher than a 20-story building! This giant truck carries 19,000 gallons of water – that's like having four backyard swimming pools full of water ready to fight fires!

26. Ever seen a snowmobile that can climb straight up a mountain? The Snowhawk 3 can drive up slopes steeper than stairs! It has special tracks that grip the snow like

thousands of tiny hands, and it can even do backflips in the air. It's like a motorcycle made specially for snow.

27. The most powerful tractor ever made is the Big Bud 747. This farming giant is wider than two regular tractors and can plow 1.3 acres of land in a single minute! That's like clearing an entire football field in less time than it takes to tie your shoes.

28. Want to hear about a really unique bus? The Dutch Amphibious Bus looks like a regular tour bus but can drive straight into water and become a boat! Tourists don't even need to get off – they just stay in their seats while the bus splashes into the canal for a water tour.

29. The longest motorcycle ever built stretched 93 feet long! Built in Italy, this bike was longer than a tennis court and could seat 25 people. It had to be steered from both the front and back, like a very long bicycle built for a whole classroom of kids!

30. The biggest Jeep in the world is five times taller than a regular Jeep! Called the Wild Boar, it stands 21 feet tall and has tires that are 10 feet high. The doors are so big they need their own motors to open and close. It's like having a monster truck pretending to be a Jeep!

Chapter Three

Famous Cars and Trucks in Movies and TV

A look at iconic vehicles like the Batmobile, Lightning McQueen, and Optimus Prime.

1. Did you know there have been seven different Batmobiles in Batman movies? The coolest one might be from "The Dark Knight" (2008), which was like a tank and a race car combined! It could jump over gaps, shoot fire from its back, and turn its wheels sideways to make super-sharp turns. The car was 15 feet long and weighed as much as three regular cars!

2. Lightning McQueen from "Cars" was designed to look like a mix of a NASCAR racer and a regular sports car. His number 95 was chosen to honor the year 1995 when the first "Toy Story" movie came out. The designers looked at over 100 real race cars before creating Lightning's special red and gold design!

3. Optimus Prime from "Transformers" transforms into a mighty Peterbilt 379 truck! In robot form, he stands 28 feet tall – as high as a three-story building. His truck form is painted with red and blue flames that took artists five days to paint. When he transforms, there are 10,108 different moving parts!

4. Remember the DeLorean time machine from "Back to the Future"? This amazing car needed to reach exactly 88 miles per hour to travel through time! The real DeLorean car had special doors that opened up instead of out, and was made of shiny stainless steel – the same material as kitchen sinks!

5. KITT from "Knight Rider" was a talking car that could drive itself and had a personality! Based on a black Pontiac Trans Am, KITT had a special red scanner light in the front that moved back and forth like a heartbeat. The car could drive at 300 miles per hour and even jump over obstacles!

6. The Mystery Machine from "Scooby-Doo" is a groovy van painted in psychedelic colors – blue, green, and orange! While it looks like a Volkswagen van, it's actually a Ford Econoline. Inside, it has everything the gang needs to solve mysteries, including a table for planning and storage for Scooby Snacks!

7. The Ghostbusters' ECTO-1 was actually an old ambulance that they turned into a ghost-catching car! It was a 1959 Cadillac Miller-Meteor with flashing lights, sirens, and all sorts of weird gadgets strapped to the roof. The car was so heavy with equipment that it often broke down during filming!

8. In "Cars," Mater the tow truck was based on a 1951 International Harvester tow truck. The rusty color on his metal came from spending years in the sun, but he can still drive backward faster than most cars can go forward! His license plate reads "A113" – a secret number that appears in many Disney movies.

9. The A-Team's van was a 1983 GMC Vandura painted black and metallic gray with a red stripe. It had cool red turbine wheels and a rear spoiler on top. Even though the bad guys shot at it in every episode, the van never seemed to get seriously damaged and always helped the team escape!

10. Bumblebee from "Transformers" started as a beat-up yellow Volkswagen Beetle, just like in the cartoon! But in the movies, he became a shiny yellow Chevrolet Camaro with black racing stripes. When he transforms into a robot, he's 16 feet tall – about as tall as a giraffe!

11. The General Lee from "The Dukes of Hazzard" was a bright orange 1969 Dodge Charger with the number 01 on the sides. It was famous for jumping over everything – cars, trucks, even rivers! During the whole TV show, they used up more than 300 different cars because they kept crashing them during stunts!

12. Herbie the Love Bug was a Volkswagen Beetle with a mind of its own! This little white car had red, white, and blue racing stripes and the number 53. Herbie could drive himself and had feelings just like a person. He could even get sad or happy! In the movies, 11 different Herbies were used.

13. The Speed Racer Mach 5 had more gadgets than a Swiss Army knife! It had special buttons that made the car jump, drive underwater, cut down trees with giant saws, and even drive up walls! The real car built for the 2008 movie cost over $1 million to make and could really drive.

14. The "Jurassic Park" Explorer was a special Ford Explorer painted green and tan with the park's logo on the side. It ran on a track through the dinosaur park and had a cool glass roof so visitors could see the dinosaurs above. The car even had a computer screen showing dinosaur facts!

15. Doc Hudson from "Cars" was based on a 1951 Hudson Hornet, a real race car that won many races in the 1950s! His dark blue color and smooth design made him look very classy. The real Hudson Hornet was nicknamed the "Fabulous Hudson Hornet" and was one of the fastest cars of its time.

16. The Pizza Planet truck from "Toy Story" is a beaten-up yellow Toyota pickup truck with a giant rocket on top! This truck has appeared in almost every Pixar movie as a hidden secret – even in movies like "Wall-E" and "Brave" where you wouldn't expect to see a modern truck!

17. The Mutt Cutts van from "Dumb and Dumber" was a Ford Econoline van made to look like a giant shaggy dog! It had fake fur all over it, floppy ears on the sides, a nose on the front, and even a wagging tail in the back. The van actually had a regular paint job underneath all that fur!

18. K.I.T.T.'s evil twin K.A.R.R. from "Knight Rider" looked almost exactly like K.I.T.T., but had a yellow scanner light instead of red. Both cars could talk and drive themselves, but K.A.R.R. was selfish and mean while K.I.T.T. was helpful and kind. It's like they were car brothers who didn't get along!

19. The "Back to the Future" train from Part III was a real steam locomotive that Doc Brown turned into a time machine! It had special wheels that could run on regular train tracks or fly through the air. The front had giant wings and rockets that helped it reach 88 miles per hour!

20. The Monkeemobile was a custom-made car for the TV show "The Monkees." It started as a 1966 Pontiac GTO but got totally changed with a wild-looking nose, a huge blower on the engine, and a special back seat that could hold all the band's musical instruments!

21. The Teenage Mutant Ninja Turtles' Party Wagon was like a rolling fortress! This green van had all sorts of weapons and gadgets hidden inside, including a pizza launcher! It was armored to protect the turtles from bad guys and even had a special sunroof for Michelangelo to throw his nunchucks through!

22. The time-traveling train from "Back to the Future Part III" was actually built from a real steam locomotive! They added lots of crazy science fiction parts to it, like special lights and a flux capacitor. The train could fly and shoot sparks, making it look like a mix between a train and a spaceship!

23. In "Transformers," Jazz turns into a super cool Pontiac Solstice sports car! When he transforms, he does breakdancing moves and can even do backflips. He's one of the smaller Autobots, about the size of two tall adults standing on each other's shoulders, but he's super fast and agile!

24. The Bluesmobile from "The Blues Brothers" was a retired police car that looked boring on the outside but was super powerful inside! It could do amazing jumps, drive through shopping malls, and even outrun the police. They used 13 different cars during filming because of all the crazy stunts!

25. The Mirthmobile from "Wayne's World" was a baby blue AMC Pacer – one of the weirdest-looking cars ever made! It had flames painted on the sides and a special roof rack for their musical instruments. The car wasn't very fast or cool, but that's what made it funny in the movie!

26. Finn McMissile from "Cars 2" is a spy car based on classic British sports cars! He has more gadgets than James Bond's car, including extendable wheel-mounted machine guns, hidden rocket launchers, and even underwater fins! His license plate changes color to help him stay undercover.

27. The Wraith car from the movie "The Wraith" was actually a Dodge M4S Turbo Interceptor! It looked so futuristic that people thought it wasn't real, but it was a real prototype car that cost $1.5 million to build. It could go from 0 to 60 miles per hour in just 4.1 seconds!

28. The car from "Chitty Chitty Bang Bang" could drive, float on water, and even fly! The real car used in the movie was 17 feet long and had brass fittings, woodwork, and a special red and cream color scheme. They actually built several versions – one for driving, one for floating, and one for flying scenes!

29. The "Mad Max" V8 Interceptor was based on a 1973 Ford Falcon XB GT from Australia! It was painted completely black and had a huge supercharger sticking out of the hood. The car became so famous that fans built hundreds of replicas, but only two original cars were used in the movies!

30. The "Cars" character Sally Carrera was designed to look like a 2002 Porsche 911! Her baby blue color was custom-made for the movie and isn't available on real Porsches. The designers gave her high headlights to look like eyebrows, making her seem more friendly and approachable than regular sports cars!

Chapter Four

From Horsepower to Electric Power

How Vehicles Have Changed Trace the journey from early steam engines to today's electric vehicles and futuristic concepts.

1. The very first cars didn't even have engines – they were pulled by horses! Called "horseless carriages," these wooden wagons had big wheels and uncomfortable wooden seats. When the first engines came along in the late 1800s, people were amazed that a carriage could

move without a horse. Many thought these "noisy machines" would never catch on!

2. Did you know that early cars had to be started with a hand crank? Before electric starters were invented in 1912, drivers had to go to the front of their car and turn a big metal handle really hard to start the engine. Sometimes the crank would suddenly spin backward and hurt people's arms – ouch!

3. The first cars actually ran on steam, just like old trains! You had to wait about 30 minutes for the steam to build up before you could drive anywhere. Imagine waiting half an hour every morning just to start your car! These steam cars needed lots of water, and they would run out after just a few miles.

4. Electric cars aren't new at all – they were popular over 100 years ago! In 1900, one-third of all cars were electric. They were especially popular with ladies because they didn't have smelly exhaust or that tricky hand crank.

But these old electric cars could only go about 20 miles before needing a recharge.

5. The first gas-powered car was built by Karl Benz in 1885, and it looked more like a three-wheeled bicycle than a car! It could only go 10 miles per hour – slower than you can ride your bike. The engine was so loud that it scared horses on the street, and people had to warn others before driving by!

6. Henry Ford's Model T changed everything about cars in 1908. Before the Model T, cars were hand-made and super expensive – only rich people could buy them. Ford created the assembly line, where each worker added one part to the car. This made cars much cheaper, and soon regular families could afford them!

7. Early car drivers had to be really brave! Cars didn't have windshields, so bugs and dust would hit drivers in the face. They wore special goggles to protect their eyes. There were no gas stations either – drivers had to buy

fuel from drugstores in small cans. Talk about a different way to fill up!

8. The first car radios appeared in the 1930s, and people thought they were dangerous! Some states wanted to ban them because they worried drivers would get too distracted by the music and crash. These early radios were huge – about the size of a modern microwave – and cost as much as a small car!

9. Seat belts weren't required in cars until the 1960s! Before that, people just slid around on the seats when the car turned corners. The first seat belts were just like the belts you wear with pants. Today's seat belts, which go across both your lap and shoulder, weren't invented until 1959.

10. Modern electric cars are super different from old ones! The Tesla Model S can go over 400 miles on one charge – that's like driving from New York City to Canada! It can also go from zero to 60 miles per hour

in just 2.3 seconds, which is faster than most race cars. No more slow electric carriages!

11. The first car heaters were really weird! In the 1920s, drivers would collect heat from the engine in blankets and wrap them around their legs to stay warm. Later, they used special boxes full of bricks heated in a fire. You had to warm up the bricks before your trip – imagine doing that on a cold morning!

12. Cars didn't always have trunks for storage. In the early days, if you wanted to carry anything, you had to strap it to the outside of the car! People would tie suitcases, boxes, and even furniture to special racks. The word "trunk" comes from the actual wooden trunks people would attach to their cars.

13. The first traffic light was installed in London in 1868, and it didn't have any electric lights! It used green and red gas lamps that a policeman had to change by hand. One day, the gas light exploded and hurt the po-

liceman. After that, they waited 50 years before trying traffic lights again!

14. Today's hybrid cars are like having two engines in one car – a regular gas engine and an electric motor! They work together like a team: the electric motor helps save gas in the city, and the gas engine takes over on highways. Some hybrids can even drive on just electricity for short trips!

15. Early windshield wipers had to be moved by hand! In 1903, Mary Anderson invented the first windshield wiper after seeing drivers stop their streetcars to clear snow. Her invention was a rubber blade attached to a lever inside the car. Drivers had to push and pull the lever while steering!

16. The first car air conditioners were blocks of ice with fans blowing over them! In the 1930s, people would put a big block of ice in a special container, and a fan would blow air over it into the car. The ice would melt

after a few hours, and you'd have to buy more. Imagine stopping for ice instead of gas!

17. Car tires used to be white! Natural rubber is white, and early tires were this color. In 1910, companies started adding carbon black to make tires stronger and last longer, which turned them black. White tires got dirty really quickly anyway – sometimes they would look brown after just one drive!

18. The first car cup holders weren't added until the 1950s! Before that, if you wanted a drink while driving, you had to balance it on your lap or the seat. Early cup holders were flimsy metal rings that hung from the car door. They would often break or spill drinks all over the car's floor.

19. Future cars might drive themselves! Many companies are working on self-driving cars that use computers, cameras, and sensors to navigate roads. These cars can see in all directions at once and never get tired or

distracted. Some even have special seats that can turn around so passengers can face each other!

20. Early cars didn't have keys! To start them, you just pushed a button. Car keys weren't common until the 1920s, when car theft became a problem. The first car keys only opened the doors – you still had to push a button to start the engine. Today's key fobs can start cars from far away!

21. Some modern cars can park themselves! They use special sensors to measure parking spaces and turn the steering wheel automatically. All the driver has to do is control the gas and brake pedals. These cars can squeeze into tight spots better than most human drivers – it's like having a robot valet!

22. The first car horns were actually whistles! They were powered by engine exhaust and made a loud shrieking sound. Later, people used bulb horns that made a "honk" sound when squeezed. Electric horns weren't

invented until 1908, and they were so loud that many cities banned them at night!

23. Today's electric cars are so quiet that they have to make fake engine sounds! This helps warn pedestrians that a car is coming. Some cars let you choose the sound – you can make your car sound like a spaceship or a regular engine. It's like having a sound effects machine in your car!

24. Cars of the future might run on hydrogen! These cars have special fuel cells that turn hydrogen gas into electricity. The only thing that comes out of the exhaust pipe is water vapor – clean enough to drink! Some buses and trucks already use this technology, and it might be common in cars soon.

25. The first car mirrors were just like bathroom mirrors! They were added in 1911, but they only showed what was behind the car. Side mirrors weren't common until the 1960s. Today's cars have special mirrors

that can dim automatically at night and even show you what's in your blind spots!

26. Modern engines are like tiny computers! They have special sensors that check everything thousands of times per second. If something goes wrong, the car's computer tells the mechanic exactly what the problem is. It's like having a doctor for your car that can instantly diagnose any issue!

27. Early cars didn't have gas gauges! Drivers had to use a stick to measure how much gas was in their tank, just like checking oil today. Sometimes they would run out of gas in the middle of nowhere! The first gas gauge wasn't invented until 1922 – before that, it was always a guessing game.

28. Cars keep getting smarter! Some new cars can read road signs, warn you if you're getting sleepy, and even stop themselves if they sense danger ahead. They have special cameras and radar that work like extra eyes,

watching all around the car to keep everyone safe. It's like having a guardian angel!

29. The first car GPS systems came with giant map books on CD-ROMs! They could only show simple maps and often got confused. Today's GPS can show 3D maps, find the fastest route around traffic jams, and even tell you where to find your favorite restaurant. It's like having a tiny tour guide in your car!

30. Flying cars might be coming soon! Several companies are building cars with folding wings or giant propellers. These vehicles could drive on roads and then take off from small airports. Some can even take off and land vertically like a helicopter! While they're still being tested, we might see them in the sky soon!

Chapter Five

Mega Machines

The Strongest Trucks and Trains
Discover the mightiest trucks and trains used for construction, transport, and more.

1. Meet the Liebherr T 282B, one of the biggest dump trucks in the world! This monster truck can carry as much weight as 365 elephants in its giant bed. Its tires are taller than two adults standing on each other's shoulders, and each one costs more than a fancy car! The driver climbs a huge ladder just to get into the cabin.

2. The world's strongest train locomotive, the Big Boy, was so powerful it could pull 100 railroad cars at once!

This steam giant was longer than three school buses and needed two separate engines to work properly. Eight of these amazing trains still exist today in museums, where their massive size amazes visitors.

3. Ever heard of the Bucket Wheel Excavator? It's the largest land vehicle ever built! This mining machine is taller than a 30-story building and as long as two football fields. Its wheel has giant buckets that can scoop up enough dirt to fill a swimming pool in just one minute! It moves using giant tank tracks.

4. The Caterpillar 797F mining truck has six tires that each cost $42,500 – that's more than many fancy cars! When fully loaded, it weighs as much as 126 elephants. Its engine is so powerful that it could power 3,400 regular cars. The truck is so tall that mechanics have to use ladders to check the engine.

5. The Antonov AN-225 cargo plane was like a flying truck! It could carry 21 regular-sized buses inside its

belly. The plane had 32 wheels to help it land safely with all that weight. Its wings were longer than a football field, and it had six giant engines to lift all that cargo into the sky!

6. The Australian Road Train is like a snake made of trucks! These mega trucks can have up to four trailers connected together, stretching longer than a football field. They carry cargo through the Australian Outback, where roads go straight for hundreds of miles. One road train can carry as much as 80 regular trucks!

7. The Crawler-Transporter used by NASA is actually a giant truck that moves rockets! It's as big as a baseball field and moves slower than a turtle – just one mile per hour. Each of its tracks has 57 shoes, and each shoe weighs as much as a car. It carries space rockets to their launch pads!

8. The Belaz 75710 dump truck is so big that its cab sits three stories high! The driver needs to climb a ladder

to reach it, like climbing to a treehouse. Its bed can hold enough rocks to fill two backyard swimming pools. When empty, it still weighs as much as 100 regular cars put together!

9. The Union Pacific Big Boy locomotive was so long it had to be designed to bend in the middle! This helped it turn around corners on mountain tracks. Its whistle was so loud it could be heard from 10 miles away! Each drive wheel was taller than a grown adult, and it needed 14 wheels on each side.

10. The LeTourneau L-2350 loader is the largest wheel loader ever built! Its bucket can lift as much weight as six elephants at once. The cabin sits so high up that it has an elevator to help the driver reach it. It's mainly used in mines to load those giant dump trucks we talked about earlier!

11. The Terex RH400 is like a giant robot arm that digs! This massive excavator can scoop up 94 tons of dirt in

one bite – that's like picking up 60 cars at once! Its cabin is so high up that it has a special camera system to help the operator see the ground. The whole machine weighs as much as 980 cars!

12. The Porsche 911 GT2 RS engine has 700 horsepower, but the Caterpillar 6090 mining truck engine has 11,300 horsepower! That's like having 16 sports cars' worth of power in one engine. It's so big that a person can stand up inside it, and it drinks enough fuel to fill a regular car's gas tank every 30 minutes!

13. The Komatsu PC8000 mining shovel is like a giant steel dinosaur! Its bucket can hold enough dirt to fill a living room. The operator sits in a cabin as big as a small bedroom, with computer screens showing every angle around the machine. Each track is longer than a car and helps it move around safely.

14. The biggest locomotive in current use, the AC6000CW, has enough power to light up 6,000

homes! It uses a special computer system to control all that power, kind of like having a giant video game controller. The engine is so strong it can pull 100 fully loaded train cars up a steep hill!

15. The Mammoet PTC 200 DS crane is as tall as a 40-story building! It can lift as much weight as 1,000 elephants and can turn all the way around like a ballerina. The crane takes 20 trucks just to deliver all its parts, and it needs a whole week to be put together!

16. The Chieftain Crab Catcher boat is like a giant floating factory! This mega fishing boat has huge cranes that can lift 150 tons of crab pots out of the ocean at once. It's longer than a football field and can stay at sea for months. The boat even has its own hospital and movie theater for the crew!

17. The Bagger 288 excavator is so huge it holds a world record! This machine is used to dig up coal and can remove enough dirt in one day to fill 2,400 trucks. It

uses electricity instead of gas and needs as much power as a small city! The machine moves on giant caterpillar tracks that spread out its weight.

18. The Overburden Conveyor Bridge F60 is like a giant moving bridge! This huge machine is used in mining and is longer than the Eiffel Tower is tall. It moves along tracks and can transport enough dirt and rock in one hour to fill an Olympic swimming pool five times! The whole thing weighs as much as 502 elephants.

19. The Liebherr LR 13000 crawler crane can lift as much weight as 11 fully loaded Boeing 747 airplanes! Its boom (the long arm that lifts things) can reach higher than the Statue of Liberty. The crane moves around on tracks like a tank, and it takes 200 trucks to move all its parts to a new location!

20. The Emma Maersk container ship is like a floating skyscraper turned on its side! This massive ship can carry 15,000 shipping containers at once – if you lined up all

those containers, they would stretch for 57 miles! The ship's engine is as tall as a four-story building and as heavy as 7,000 cars.

21. The Hitachi EX8000 excavator is like a giant mechanical arm with a bucket that could fill your bedroom with dirt in one scoop! The operator sits in a cabin bigger than most bathrooms, with air conditioning and computers to control the machine. Each track is longer than a school bus!

22. The Sikorsky Skycrane helicopter is like a flying truck! This special helicopter can lift cars, boats, and even smaller helicopters! It has six giant rotor blades and can carry up to 20,000 pounds – that's like lifting four elephants at once! Firefighters use it to carry huge tanks of water to fight forest fires.

23. The Komatsu D575A bulldozer is the biggest in the world! Its blade is wider than two cars parked side by side and can push enough dirt to fill six dump trucks in

one go. The driver sits 16 feet above the ground – higher than a basketball hoop! It weighs as much as 12 fully loaded school buses.

24. The Liebherr R 9800 mining excavator has a bucket so big it could hold three cars! This mega machine weighs more than a thousand elephants and needs five different engines to power it. The cabin has special cameras that give the operator a view all around the machine, like having eyes in the back of their head!

25. The CAT 994K wheel loader is like a giant forklift on steroids! Its bucket can lift as much as eight full-grown elephants at once. The tires are twice as tall as a grown adult, and each one costs more than a fancy sports car. It's used in mines to load those massive dump trucks we talked about earlier!

26. The Terex MT 6300AC mining truck can carry enough rock to fill your entire classroom! Its fuel tank holds enough diesel to drive a regular car around the

Earth twice. The truck is so tall that workers need to climb 20 steps just to reach the driver's seat – it's like climbing to the top of a playground slide!

27. The Union Pacific GTELs were like jet engines on wheels! These special locomotives used airplane engines to power trains. They were so loud that towns would complain when they passed through! Each one could pull a train two miles long and used so much fuel they eventually had to stop using them.

28. The Volvo L350H wheel loader has a special computer brain that helps it work smarter! It can lift as much as five cars at once and has shock absorbers like a giant mountain bike. The cabin is super comfortable with a special seat that turns around so the operator can see in all directions.

29. The Manitowoc 31000 crawler crane is like having a metal giraffe that can lift entire buildings! It can reach higher than a 30-story building and lift as much as 2,500

cars at once. The crane is so big that it builds itself – it has special motors that help put its own pieces together!

30. The Bucyrus RH400 mining shovel can fill three mining trucks in just five minutes! Its bucket is big enough to park a car inside, and each tooth on the bucket weighs as much as a grown person. The operator sits in a glass cabin that's higher than a two-story house and uses joysticks to control this metal giant!

Chapter Six

Wild Wheels

The Weirdest and Wackiest Cars and Trucks Highlight unique vehicles with unusual designs, like monster trucks, hovercrafts, and amphibious cars.

1. Have you heard of the Amphicar? It's a car that can drive right into water and become a boat! Built in the 1960s, this crazy vehicle had special watertight doors and a propeller hidden underneath. When it reached water, the driver would just drive in, turn on the propeller, and cruise around like a regular boat!

2. The Lunar Roving Vehicle was like a dune buggy for astronauts on the Moon! It had special wire mesh wheels because regular rubber tires wouldn't work in space. The car could drive over moon rocks and craters

while folding up small enough to fit in the lunar landing module. Talk about an out-of-this-world ride!

3. Monster Jam trucks are like giant toy cars come to life! These massive trucks have tires taller than most adults and engines with over 1,500 horsepower. They can jump higher than a two-story house and do backflips! Each truck goes through about 8 sets of tires every year because of all their crazy stunts.

4. The Rinspeed sQuba is a car that can drive underwater like a submarine! This modern car can dive up to 33 feet deep and has special electric motors that work under water. The passengers even have to wear scuba gear because the cabin fills with water. It's like something from a James Bond movie!

5. The Helicron was a weird French car from 1932 that used a giant propeller to move forward! Instead of regular wheels pushing it along, this car had an airplane propeller on the front that pulled it down the road. The

driver had to be careful because the spinning propeller could chop up anything in its way!

6. Meet the longest car in the world – the American Dream limousine! This crazy car is 100 feet long and has 26 wheels. It includes a swimming pool, a diving board, a king-sized bed, and even a helipad for landing helicopters! The car is so long it needs two drivers – one in the front and one in the back.

7. The Moller Skycar looks like a flying saucer with wheels! This flying car has four powerful fans that let it take off and land vertically like a helicopter. While it hasn't been approved for regular use yet, the inventors say it could fly at 375 miles per hour and drive on regular roads when it's not flying.

8. The Gibbs Aquada is a sports car that turns into a speedboat in just 12 seconds! When it reaches water, the wheels fold up into the body and a jet drive takes over. This fancy vehicle can go 100 miles per hour on land

and 30 miles per hour in water. Virgin founder Richard Branson used one to cross the English Channel!

9. The SHERP ATV is like a monster truck mixed with a tank! It has huge hollow tires that help it float on water and climb over obstacles taller than cars. This Russian vehicle can drive up steps, crush through ice, and roll over logs. It's so tough it can keep driving even if it gets a flat tire!

10. The Hover Van is exactly what it sounds like – a regular van turned into a hovercraft! Created for a TV show, this wild vehicle floats on a cushion of air and can glide over water, snow, or sand. The back doors had to be sealed shut to keep the air cushion working, but who needs doors when you're hovering?

11. The Double-Ender car had steering wheels at both ends! Built in the 1950s, this weird car could drive in either direction without turning around. It was perfect for places with narrow streets because you never had

to make a U-turn. Imagine confusing other drivers by switching seats and driving the opposite way!

12. The Rinspeed X-Trem is a sports car with a built-in helicopter pad! This Swiss concept car has a special platform that slides out the back to carry a small helicopter. The car itself looks like something from the future, with sleek lines and doors that open upward like wings. It's like having two vehicles in one!

13. The Tracked Hummer was a regular Hummer turned into a tank! Instead of wheels, it uses tank tracks to drive over snow, mud, and rough terrain. Each track is as wide as a regular car tire and helps the vehicle float on top of deep snow. It's like having a luxury tank for winter driving!

14. The Marauder is a giant armored car that's so tough it can survive an explosion! This South African vehicle weighs as much as five regular cars and can protect passengers from almost anything. It's so tall that regular

drive-through restaurants had to turn it away – the car wouldn't fit under their roofs!

15. The TerraCross is an inflatable car that can float! This rescue vehicle has special airbags built into its body that can inflate in seconds, turning it into a boat. It was designed to help during floods and can carry up to ten people across water. When it's done floating, it deflates and drives like a normal car!

16. The PAC-CAR II holds the record for being the most fuel-efficient vehicle ever! This tiny car can travel 12,665 miles on a single gallon of gas – that's like driving halfway around the world! It looks like a spaceship on wheels and is so light that a child could lift it. The driver has to lie down inside to drive it.

17. The Shadow Hawk is a car that can transform into a plane in three minutes! The wings fold out from the sides, and the tail unfolds from the back. When it's in car mode, it looks like a regular sports car, but it can

take off from any small airport. It's like having your own personal Transformer!

18. The Bathtub Car is exactly what it sounds like – a real bathtub with wheels and an engine! Built by a car enthusiast, it has working water taps and can drive on regular roads. The driver sits in the tub and steers with a small wheel. It even has a shower head attached to spray water while driving!

19. The WaterCar Panther can go from road to river faster than you can tie your shoes! This Jeep-like vehicle has a special water jet engine that kicks in when it enters the water. On land, it can go faster than most sports cars, and in water, it's speedier than many boats. It's perfect for beach adventures!

20. The LITEcar glows in the dark! This electric concept car has special panels that light up different colors. The whole car can change color like a chameleon, and the lights can display messages to other drivers. At night,

it looks like a rolling rainbow! The lights also make it super visible for safety.

21. The Spider Car has eight legs instead of wheels! Created by a British inventor, this wild vehicle walks instead of rolls. Each leg has its own motor, and the car can step over obstacles that would stop regular cars. It moves kind of like a giant mechanical spider, which makes it perfect for rough terrain.

22. The Schwimmwagen was a car from World War II that could swim! Built by Volkswagen, it had a watertight body and a propeller that could be lowered into the water. When driving on land, the propeller folded up against the back of the car. Soldiers used it to cross rivers and lakes during the war.

23. The Stout Scarab was like a living room on wheels! Built in the 1930s, this weird-looking car had seats that could turn around and even a small table inside. The engine was in the back, and the front looked like a bee-

tle's head. It was one of the first minivans ever made, but only nine were built!

24. The Hoverboard Car looks like something from "Back to the Future"! This concept car has special magnetic wheels that could let it hover a few inches off the ground. While it's still just an idea, the designers want it to float over special magnetic roads. Imagine never hitting a pothole again!

25. The DUCK (Designated Underwater Cruising Kolossus) is a bus that turns into a boat! These amphibious vehicles take tourists on city tours that splash right into rivers or harbors. The passengers stay dry while the bus cruises through the water like a boat. It's like having a bus and a boat tour in one trip!

26. The Cycle Car is a car powered by bicycle pedals! This eco-friendly vehicle lets four people pedal together to make it move. It has a small electric motor to help on hills, but most of the power comes from the riders' legs.

It's like a bicycle built for four people with a roof to keep out the rain!

27. The Snow Crawler has tank tracks wider than a person! This giant vehicle is used in Antarctica to cross huge fields of ice and snow. The cabin is heated and can sleep six people comfortably. It's like a tiny house on tracks that can drive through the coldest places on Earth!

28. The Rolling Sphere Car is shaped like a giant ball! This bizarre vehicle has one big wheel that wraps around the entire car. The driver sits in a capsule in the middle that stays level while the outer wheel rolls. It's like being inside a hamster ball that you can drive! Sadly, it never made it past the test phase.

29. The Bubble Car was a tiny car that looked like a space pod! Made in the 1950s, these cute little cars had a door that opened at the front like a refrigerator. They were so light that strong winds could blow them

around, and some people say they would float in deep puddles! Only three wheels kept them rolling.

30. The Rocket Car uses actual jet engines to move! Built for breaking speed records, this car has airplane engines attached to it. It can go faster than some planes and leaves a trail of fire behind it when the engines are on full power. The driver has to wear a special suit just like airplane pilots!

Chapter Seven

Train Routes Around the World

Scenic and Historic Rides Fun facts on famous train routes like Japan's Shinkansen, the Rocky Mountaineer, and the Orient Express.

1. Japan's Shinkansen bullet trains look like sleek white birds zooming through the country! These amazing trains can travel at 200 miles per hour – faster than some small airplanes. They're so punctual that if they're more than one minute late, it makes the news! The average delay is only 54 seconds. That's super precise!

2. The Rocky Mountaineer train in Canada has special glass-domed cars where you can see the mountains above you! As the train winds through the Canadian Rockies, passengers can spot bears, eagles, and mountain goats from their seats. The train even slows down for the best views and wildlife photos!

3. The original Orient Express was like a fancy hotel on wheels! Kings and queens used to ride this train from Paris to Istanbul. The dining cars had crystal glasses and silver plates, and the seats were covered in soft velvet. It took about three days to complete the journey, and passengers dressed up for dinner every night!

4. The Flåm Railway in Norway is one of the steepest regular train rides in the world! It climbs 2,833 feet up through beautiful mountains and passes by 20 tunnels and one of the most powerful waterfalls in Norway. The trip only takes an hour, but the train has to use special brakes to stay safe on the steep tracks!

5. Switzerland's Glacier Express is called the slowest express train in the world! But that's because it goes through such beautiful mountain scenery that it needs to take its time. The train crosses 291 bridges and goes through 91 tunnels. The windows are extra large and curved so you can see the mountaintops!

6. The Trans-Siberian Railway is the longest train route in the world! It takes 7 days to travel from Moscow to Vladivostok, crossing 8 time zones. That's like taking a week-long train ride through seven different bedtimes! The train passes through the Ural Mountains and around the world's deepest lake.

7. India's Toy Train to Darjeeling is tiny but mighty! This little train chugs up mountains so steep that it has to make loops and zigzags to climb them. Sometimes it gets so close to buildings that passengers could reach out and shake hands with people in their homes! The track is only 2 feet wide.

8. The Palace on Wheels in India is like riding in a maharaja's palace! Each train car is decorated like a royal room, with beautiful carpets and fancy furniture. The train even has a spa and gym onboard. Every passenger gets their own butler to bring them snacks and drinks throughout the eight-day journey!

9. Australia's Ghan train travels through the Outback from Adelaide to Darwin! The journey takes three days and covers almost 2,000 miles. Passengers can see kangaroos hopping alongside the train and red deserts stretching as far as they can see. The train is named after the Afghan cameleers who first explored this route.

10. The Kuranda Scenic Railway in Australia winds through a rainforest that's 130 million years old! The train passes by waterfalls and travels over 37 bridges made of steel and wood. Sometimes the train goes through clouds because it climbs so high into the mountains. It took 1,500 men five years to build this track!

11. Peru's train to Machu Picchu zigzags up the Andes Mountains like a snake! The train has to make special switchback turns to climb the steep mountain. Passengers can see ancient Incan ruins and llamas grazing on the mountainsides. The train's windows are designed so you can look straight up at the peaks!

12. The Pride of Africa train is like a time machine on wheels! This luxury train travels through several African countries in vintage cars from the 1920s. Passengers dine on crystal plates while watching giraffes and elephants walk by their windows. Some trips last up to 15 days, like a cruise ship on land!

13. The West Highland Line in Scotland passes by the lake where people look for the Loch Ness Monster! The train crosses a famous viaduct that looks like something from a Harry Potter movie – because it is! The Glenfinnan Viaduct appears in the films when the Hogwarts Express carries students to school.

14. The Bernina Express in Switzerland climbs higher than any other regular train in Europe! It goes up to 7,391 feet above sea level, where passengers can see glaciers and snow-capped peaks all year round. The train's windows are extra large and stretch up into the roof so you can see everything!

15. China's high-speed trains are like silver bullets shooting across the country! They can travel at 350 kilometers per hour (that's 217 miles per hour). The trains are so smooth that you can balance a coin on its edge while zooming along. They connect major cities like Beijing and Shanghai in just 4.5 hours!

16. The Durango & Silverton Railroad in Colorado still uses steam engines from the 1880s! The train chugs through canyons so steep that passengers feel like they're floating above the river below. The track is so narrow in places that it looks like the train is riding along the edge of a cliff!

17. The Venice Simplon-Orient-Express train has a piano bar where musicians play while the train rolls through Europe! The train cars are over 100 years old and decorated with beautiful wood panels and art from the 1920s. Passengers dress up in fancy clothes for dinner, just like people did 100 years ago!

18. The TranzAlpine train in New Zealand crosses from one side of the South Island to the other in just 4.5 hours! It goes through 16 tunnels, over 4 viaducts, and past rivers that are bright blue from glacier water. The train has an open-air viewing car where you can feel the mountain breeze!

19. The Golden Eagle Trans-Siberian Express has a doctor traveling on board at all times! This luxury train takes two weeks to cross Russia, and each cabin has heated floors and its own bathroom. The train even has a professor who gives talks about the places they pass through, like a moving classroom!

20. The Maharajas' Express in India has bathrooms made of gold and marble! This super fancy train has restaurants that serve food on golden plates. Each cabin has its own mini-fridge and big windows with curtains made of silk. It's like staying in a five-star hotel that moves across India!

21. The Train to the Clouds in Argentina climbs so high that passengers might feel dizzy! The track reaches 13,842 feet above sea level – higher than most mountains in Europe. The train has oxygen masks available because the air gets so thin. It crosses 29 bridges and goes through 21 tunnels!

22. The Copper Canyon train in Mexico travels through canyons deeper than the Grand Canyon! The train takes 16 hours to complete its journey and crosses 37 bridges and goes through 86 tunnels. Some parts of the canyon are so deep that you can't see the bottom from the train windows!

23. The Eastern & Oriental Express travels through three countries in Southeast Asia! The train has a special observation car at the back where passengers can watch the sunset over rice fields and jungles. The dining car serves foods from Thailand, Malaysia, and Singapore as the train passes through each country!

24. The Royal Scotsman train is like a Scottish castle on wheels! Only 36 passengers can ride at once, making it one of the smallest luxury trains in the world. The train stops at castles and whisky distilleries, and every night bagpipe players perform for the passengers. Each room even has its own shower!

25. The Blue Train in South Africa has special windows that change color in the sunlight! The train takes 27 hours to travel between Pretoria and Cape Town, and all the food is served on fine china plates. Each cabin has a special button you can press to call your own personal butler!

26. Japan's Hello Kitty bullet train is painted pink and white with Hello Kitty pictures everywhere! Even the seats and food are Hello Kitty themed. The train goes so fast that mountains look like they're zooming past in a blur. It's like riding in a cartoon that moves at 200 miles per hour!

27. The Rocky Mountain Express in Canada uses a steam engine that's almost 100 years old! The engine makes big puffs of steam as it climbs through mountain passes. Passengers can see bears fishing in rivers and mountain goats climbing on cliffs right from their windows. It's like riding through a nature documentary!

28. The Al Andalus train in Spain is nicknamed the Palace on Wheels of Spain! The train cars were built in the 1920s and have beautiful wooden walls and crystal chandeliers. The train travels through Spain's most famous cities, and chefs come aboard to teach passengers how to cook Spanish food!

29. The Qinghai-Tibet Railway is the highest train route in the world! The train cars have special oxygen systems because they travel so high up in the mountains. Passengers can see wild yaks and antelopes running across the Tibetan plateau. Some parts of the track are built on permanent ice!

30. The Northern Lights Train in Alaska is designed for watching the aurora borealis! The train has special clear domed cars so passengers can look up at the colorful lights dancing in the sky. The train turns off its lights when the northern lights appear, and a guide explains the science behind the light show!

Chapter Eight

Off-Road Adventure Machines

SUVs, Monster Trucks, and All-Terrain Vehicles Exciting vehicles made for rugged terrains, from deserts to mountains.

1. Meet the Jeep Wrangler Rubicon, the king of rock climbing cars! This tough SUV has special tires as tall as a third-grader and can drive through three feet of water without getting stuck. It has a special system called "Rock-Trac" that lets each wheel move separately over big rocks, like a mountain goat climbing steep cliffs!

2. Grave Digger is one of the most famous monster trucks ever! Its giant tires are 66 inches tall – that's taller than most adults. The truck can jump over 30 feet in the air and crush cars like they're made of paper. With 1,500 horsepower, it's like having the power of 15 regular cars in one massive machine!

3. The Can-Am Maverick X3 is like a go-kart on steroids! This all-terrain vehicle can zoom through deserts at 87 miles per hour and jump over sand dunes like a desert kangaroo. It has special shock absorbers that work like super-strong springs, helping it bounce over bumps without shaking the riders too much.

4. The Mercedes G-Wagon was originally built for the military but became a favorite of off-road adventurers! It can climb slopes steeper than stairs and has three special locks in its wheels that help it crawl over huge rocks. The inside is as fancy as a luxury car, but it's tough enough to drive through jungles!

5. The Polaris RZR is an ATV that can drive through mud deeper than a bathtub! Its special wheels can spin independently, helping it crawl out of sticky situations. The seats are waterproof because riders often get splashed with mud, and it has lights brighter than ten flashlights for nighttime adventures!

6. The Sherp ATV looks like a tiny tank! This Russian-made vehicle has huge hollow tires that help it float on water and climb over obstacles five feet tall. It can drive through deep snow, swim across lakes, and even roll over logs. The tires are so big that they work like paddles in the water!

7. The Ford Raptor is like a pickup truck with superpowers! It was inspired by desert racing trucks and can jump over sand dunes at 100 miles per hour. The truck has special sensors that tell it when it's flying through the air, and it adjusts its shock absorbers for a smooth landing – just like a cat!

8. Monster Jam's Maximum Destruction (Max-D) looks like a silver spaceship on giant wheels! This monster truck is covered in spikes and can do perfect front flips in the air. The driver sits in a special safety cage because the truck often lands upside down after jumps. It can crush 30 cars in one show!

9. The Arctic Cat Wildcat XX is built for racing through the roughest deserts! It has three seats side-by-side and suspension that can handle jumps longer than a school bus. The special roof keeps dust out while racing, and it has a screen that shows you if any parts need fixing – like a doctor for your vehicle!

10. The Land Rover Defender can drive up mountains that are too steep to walk up! It was first built to help farmers reach places regular cars couldn't go. The newest version has a computer that can figure out what kind of ground you're driving on (like mud, snow, or rocks) and adjusts the wheels to match!

11. The Yamaha YXZ1000R is like a sports car mixed with a dune buggy! It has a special gear shift like a race car and can spray through mud puddles at 80 miles per hour. The seats are designed to hold you in place when the vehicle tilts sideways on steep hills – sometimes at angles steeper than a slide!

12. The Ram TRX is the most powerful pickup truck ever made for off-roading! It has 702 horsepower – that's like having two regular trucks combined into one. It can jump over desert bumps at 100 miles per hour and has special cooling systems to keep the engine from getting too hot in the desert.

13. The Can-Am Outlander is an ATV that can pull as much weight as a small car! It has special mud tires that are designed to clean themselves while spinning, shooting mud away from the wheels. The handle grips heat up to keep your hands warm when riding in cold weather – like having tiny heaters in your gloves!

14. The Polaris General is half work truck, half play machine! It can carry heavy loads like lumber and tools but can also race through trails at 60 miles per hour. It has a special roof that lets you listen to music through built-in speakers, and the seats are designed to stay dry even when you're splashing through rivers!

15. The Hummer H1 is so wide it barely fits on regular roads! Originally made for the military, it can drive through water up to your shoulders deep. The tires can still work even if they're shot with bullets, and it has hooks strong enough to lift the whole vehicle by helicopter – like a real-life action movie car!

16. BJ Baldwin's Trophy Truck looks like a regular pickup truck with super powers! It can jump the length of a football field and land safely on its massive shock absorbers. The truck has 850 horsepower and special computers that control each wheel separately, helping it bounce over desert bumps at highway speeds!

17. The Honda Talon lives up to its bird-of-prey name! This side-by-side ATV can climb rock walls that look impossible to drive up. It has special sensors that tell the engine exactly how much power each wheel needs, like having a tiny brain controlling each tire. The seats are designed like race car seats for safety!

18. The Mahindra Roxor looks like a tiny Jeep from World War II! This modern off-roader is built like a mini tank, with a steel body and simple design that's easy to fix if something breaks. It's so tough that many farmers use it instead of tractors, and it can pull three times its own weight!

19. The Kawasaki Teryx KRX 1000 has a special computer that helps prevent it from flipping over! It can tell when you're tilted too far and will cut power to keep you safe. The cabin is built like a safety cage, protecting riders even if the vehicle rolls over, and it has seats that can be adjusted while wearing muddy gloves!

20. The Tesla Cybertruck (coming soon) looks like something from a sci-fi movie! This electric off-roader has bulletproof windows and a body made of super-strong stainless steel. It can tow more than most pickup trucks and has special air suspension that can make it taller or shorter at the push of a button!

21. The Jeep Gladiator Mojave is specially made for racing through deserts! It has extra-strong shock absorbers that won't overheat even after hours of jumping over sand dunes. The truck bed is perfect for carrying dirt bikes or camping gear, and it has special screens that show you exactly how the vehicle is tilted!

22. The Textron Wildcat XX is built like a race car for the dirt! It has special armor protecting its bottom from rocks and can go from zero to 60 miles per hour in just a few seconds. The seats are designed to keep you com-

fortable even after hours of bouncing through rough terrain – like having a comfy couch in a race car!

23. The Polaris Ranger can work as hard as it plays! This utility task vehicle (UTV) can carry 1,000 pounds in its cargo bed – that's like carrying five dirt bikes at once! It has a special mode for crawling over rocks super slowly and safely, and the whole vehicle can be hosed down after getting muddy.

24. The Ford Bronco Raptor is built to jump sand dunes like a desert race truck! It has special reinforced parts underneath to protect it when landing big jumps, and the body is extra wide to help it stay stable in corners. The tires are designed to "float" on sand like snowshoes help you walk on snow!

25. The Arctic Cat HDX is like a Swiss Army knife with wheels! This UTV can switch from working on a farm to racing through trails in minutes. It has a special dump

bed that can lift itself up to unload cargo, and the seats can flip around to make a workbench when you need to fix something in the field!

26. The Troller T4 is a Brazilian off-road beast that can drive through rainforests! It's built to handle deep mud and river crossings, with special snorkels that help it breathe even when water is up to the hood. The body is made of plastic that won't rust, perfect for wet jungle adventures!

27. The Yamaha Wolverine RMAX is like having a mountain goat with an engine! It can climb over huge rocks and through deep mud without getting stuck. The special roof keeps rain off while still letting fresh air in, and it has a winch strong enough to pull itself out of almost any sticky situation!

28. The Can-Am Commander can switch from work mode to play mode in seconds! It has a special key that changes how the engine works – one setting for sav-

ing fuel while working, another for maximum power while playing. The cargo bed can dump like a tiny dump truck, perfect for moving dirt or camping gear!

29. The GMC Hummer EV is an electric monster that can drive sideways! It has a special "Crab Walk" mode where all four wheels turn in the same direction, letting it slide sideways around obstacles. With three electric motors, it's more powerful than most monster trucks and can raise itself up by six inches at the push of a button!

30. The Polaris Sportsman ATV has special sensors that can tell when you're going downhill! It automatically helps you brake safely, like having a robot assistant keeping you steady. The headlights turn when you turn the handlebars, helping you see around corners at night, and the seat has special storage compartments that stay dry even in rain!

Chapter Nine

How Traffic Works

Lights, Signs, and the Rules of the Road Learn how traffic systems and signs keep cars, trucks, and trains moving safely.

1. Traffic lights are like the bosses of intersections! The first electric traffic light was installed in 1914 in Cleveland, Ohio, and only had red and green lights. Yellow wasn't added until later when people realized cars needed time to slow down. Modern traffic lights are controlled by computers that can sense how many cars are waiting!

2. Did you know that STOP signs are octagons (eight-sided) so drivers can recognize them even when they're covered in snow? They're also the only eight-sided signs on the road! The bright red color was chosen because it can be seen from far away, and the white letters reflect car headlights at night.

3. School zone signs are bright yellow-green because scientists discovered this is the color our eyes notice first! These signs use special reflective paint that seems to glow in headlights. Some even have flashing lights that turn on automatically when school starts and ends. It's like having a safety guard that never gets tired!

4. Traffic roundabouts are like merry-go-rounds for cars! They help traffic flow better than regular intersections because cars don't have to stop completely. Studies show that roundabouts reduce accidents by 90% because cars have to slow down to go around the circle. Some countries call them "carousels" or "traffic circles"!

5. Smart traffic lights have special cameras that can count cars like a robot! When too many cars are waiting at a red light, the computer tells the light to turn green sooner. Some lights can even detect emergency vehicles and change to green automatically when ambulances or fire trucks are coming. Cool, right?

6. Railroad crossing signals are like a high-tech alarm system! When a train is coming, special sensors in the tracks send electrical signals that make the gates go down and the lights flash. The bells ring exactly 20 seconds before the train arrives. That's why the gates have zigzag stripes – to make them super visible!

7. Speed bumps are like little hills in the road that make cars slow down! They're designed to be just tall enough to be uncomfortable if you drive too fast, but safe if you go slowly. Some are painted with bright yellow stripes that look like tiny zebra crossings. The fancy name for speed bumps is "traffic calming devices"!

8. Traffic signs use special colors to tell drivers what they mean! Red means stop or don't do something, yellow means warning, green means go or allowed, and blue signs give information. It's like a secret color code for drivers! Brown signs usually point to parks or historic places, like a treasure map for tourists!

9. School crossing guards are like human traffic lights! They wear bright reflective vests that can be seen from really far away, and their STOP paddles are the same size as regular STOP signs. Many crossing guards learn special hand signals that mean the same thing in any language, so everyone knows what to do!

10. Some crosswalks have special buttons that make a chirping sound when it's safe to cross! These sounds help blind people know when to walk. Different countries use different sounds – in Japan, the crosswalk plays bird songs, while in Australia, it makes a clicking noise like a cricket! How cool is that?

11. Highway express lanes are like special race tracks for cars that want to go faster! Some have special gates that only open if you have a special pass, and others change direction depending on the time of day. During morning rush hour, they might go toward the city, and in the evening, they switch to going away from the city!

12. Street sweepers are like giant vacuum cleaners for roads! They have special spinning brushes that can pick up tiny pieces of trash and dirt. Many modern street sweepers have computers that remember which streets they've already cleaned, kind of like a robot vacuum cleaner for cities! They even spray water to keep dust down.

13. Some cities have special tunnels just for delivery trucks! These underground roads help keep big trucks off regular streets where they might get stuck in traffic. The tunnels have special height sensors that warn trucks if they're too tall to fit, and some even have their own traffic lights and signs!

14. Traffic cops use special hand signals that mean the same thing all over the world! When they hold both arms out, it means stop. One arm up means go. These signals work even if traffic lights aren't working! In some countries, traffic cops stand on special platforms so everyone can see them better.

15. Road reflectors are like cats' eyes for the street! They use the same technology that makes cats' eyes glow in the dark. When your headlights shine on them, they reflect the light back to help you see the road lines at night. Some even change color depending on which direction you're driving!

16. Some cities have special bridges just for animals to cross highways safely! Called wildlife overpasses, these bridges are covered with trees and grass so animals feel comfortable using them. Motion sensors count how many animals cross, and cameras have caught deer, bears, and even mountain lions using these special crosswalks!

17. Parking meters are like time machines for your car! Modern meters can send text messages when your time is running out, and some can sense when a car leaves so the next driver doesn't pay for unused time. Some smart meters even change their prices based on how busy the street is – just like surge pricing for parking!

18. Special paint used for road lines has tiny glass beads mixed in! These beads reflect light from your headlights, making the lines glow at night. The paint is also super thick – about as thick as a nickel standing on its edge – so it doesn't wear away quickly when cars drive over it.

19. Emergency vehicles have special transmitters that can change traffic lights to green! The system is called traffic signal preemption, but firefighters call it the "green light go" system. When ambulances or fire trucks turn on their sirens, nearby traffic lights automatically change to help them get through intersections safely!

20. Some crosswalks have special 3D paint that makes them look like they're floating above the road! This trick makes drivers pay more attention and slow down. The stripes appear to rise up from the road like blocks, but it's just an optical illusion. Some cities even paint them to look like piano keys!

21. Smart road signs can change their messages depending on the weather or traffic! These electronic signs use special light-up dots (like a giant calculator display) to show different warnings. They can tell drivers about accidents ahead, bad weather, or even how long it will take to reach the next exit!

22. Traffic circles in some countries have special rules about which lane to use! In the UK, drivers learn the "lane discipline" rule: use the outer lane if you're taking the first exit, and the inner lane if you're going further around. It's like a dance where everyone knows the steps!

23. Some cities have special bike traffic lights that give cyclists a head start! These lights turn green a few seconds before the regular traffic lights, helping bikes get safely through intersections before cars start moving. The bike signals often have little bicycle-shaped lights instead of regular circles!

24. Rumble strips are like music for your tires! These grooves in the road make your car vibrate and create a loud noise if you drive over them, warning you if you're getting too close to the edge of the road. They're especially helpful at night or in bad weather when it's harder to see the lines.

25. School buses have more safety features than any other vehicle! The flashing lights on top are called "eight-light warning systems" because there are eight lights total. The stop sign that swings out is called a "crossing control arm," and the front crossing gate is nicknamed the "kid catcher" because it keeps children in the driver's view!

26. Some roads have special sensors that can tell when ice is forming! These smart roads have temperature sensors built into the pavement that can trigger warning signs or even activate special heating systems to melt ice before it becomes dangerous. It's like having a winter safety guard built into the road!

27. Highway message boards use special easy-to-read letters! The font is called "Clearview" and was designed to be readable from far away, even when driving at high speeds. Each letter is shaped to prevent confusion – for example, the lowercase 'l' and uppercase 'I' look different to avoid mix-ups.

28. Some intersections have special "countdown timers" that show how long until the light changes! These timers help people decide if they have time to cross the street safely. Studies show that these counters actually reduce accidents because people aren't tempted to rush across at the last second!

29. Traffic cones are orange because it's the color that stands out most in all types of weather! The cone shape makes them stable but also easy to move, and they're made of flexible plastic so they don't damage cars if they get hit. Some modern cones have lights inside that make them glow at night!

30. Emergency shoulders on highways have special rough pavement that makes noise when you drive on it! This helps alert sleepy drivers if they drift off the road. The shoulder is also built stronger than regular lanes because it needs to support the weight of heavy trucks that might need to stop there!

Chapter Ten

Dream Cars of the Future

Self-Driving Cars, Flying Cars, and Beyond A peek into the future of transportation with autonomous and flying car concepts.

1. Self-driving cars have special cameras that act like extra eyes! These cars can see in all directions at once and can spot things humans might miss. They use computer brains to make over 1,000 decisions every second – that's faster than you can blink! Some can even see through fog and rain better than human drivers.

2. Flying cars are becoming real! The PAL-V Liberty looks like a normal car but can transform into a heli-

copter in just 10 minutes. Its rotors fold up when driving on roads, and it can fly at 112 miles per hour in the air. You'll need both a driver's license and a pilot's license to operate it!

3. The Mercedes Vision AVTR can drive sideways like a crab! This futuristic car has wheels that can turn 90 degrees, letting it move in any direction. The car connects to your brain using special sensors that can tell what you're thinking – if you think "turn right," the car turns right. It's like having a telepathic car!

4. Some future cars will be able to change color like chameleons! BMW has shown a car covered in special panels that can switch from white to black instantly. The panels work like electronic paper (like a Kindle), using tiny particles that move when given an electrical charge. Imagine changing your car color to match your mood!

5. Autonomous cars might not need steering wheels in the future! Companies are designing cars with living room-style seating where everyone faces each other. The windows can turn into TV screens for watching movies while the car drives itself. It's like having a tiny moving living room!

6. Flying taxis are being tested in cities around the world! These electric aircraft look like giant drones and can take off and land vertically like helicopters. They're much quieter than helicopters and can carry up to four passengers. Some companies plan to start flying people around cities as soon as 2025!

7. Solar-powered cars are getting better every year! The Lightyear 0 can drive for months without plugging in, using solar panels built into its roof and hood. On sunny days, it can add up to 43 miles of driving range just by sitting in a parking lot. It's like having a car that makes its own fuel from sunshine!

8. Some future cars will be able to talk to each other! Using special radio waves, cars will warn each other about accidents, bad weather, or traffic jams ahead. They can also work together to prevent traffic jams by coordinating their speeds. It's like having a whole network of cars that are best friends!

9. Underwater cars aren't just in James Bond movies anymore! Companies are developing cars with special sealed cabins and propellers that can drive on roads and underwater. Some can dive up to 33 feet deep and have oxygen tanks for the passengers. Imagine driving through an underwater tunnel and seeing fish swim by!

10. The Terrafugia TF-X is a flying car that can take off from your driveway! It has folding wings and rotors that tilt up for vertical takeoff. The car can fly itself to your destination using GPS, and if something goes wrong, it has a giant parachute that can safely lower the whole car to the ground!

11. Future cars might clean the air as they drive! Some concept cars have special filters that suck in dirty air and release clean air – like a giant air purifier on wheels. The NamX car even uses special paint that breaks down air pollution when sunlight hits it. Your car could help make cities cleaner!

12. Hyperloop pods might replace some cars and trains! These pods travel through special tubes at nearly the speed of speed of sound. They float on magnets to reduce friction and could take you from Los Angeles to San Francisco in just 30 minutes! It's like having a super-fast train that flies through a tube.

13. Some future cars will be made from materials that can repair themselves! If the car gets scratched, special chemicals in the paint can flow into the scratch and harden, making it disappear. Some companies are even working on metal that can fix small dents on its own, like having a car with healing powers!

14. The GM EN-V is a tiny electric car that can balance on two wheels like a Segway! It's designed for crowded cities and can turn around in a space smaller than a parking spot. The car can also drive itself and fold up to take less space when parked. Three EN-Vs can fit in one normal parking space!

15. Future cars might have windows that turn into touchscreens! You could tap the window to check the weather, get directions, or even order food for delivery to your next stop. Some windows could also darken automatically when it's sunny, like giant sunglasses for your car!

16. The AeroMobil flying car has wings that fold up like a butterfly! When driving, it looks like a sleek sports car, but the wings unfold for flight in less than three minutes. It can fly at 160 miles per hour and drive at normal highway speeds. The company plans to start selling them soon!

17. Some future cars will be able to charge wirelessly! Special pads built into parking spots or even roads will charge the car's batteries without any plugs. You could charge your car just by parking in the right spot or driving on certain lanes. It's like having a giant wireless phone charger for your car!

18. The Renault MORPHOZ can stretch like a rubber band! This concept car can make itself longer for highway driving (for better aerodynamics) and shorter for city parking. The inside of the car also changes shape, giving you more cargo space when needed. Imagine having a car that grows and shrinks on command!

19. Flying ambulances are being developed to reach emergencies faster! These autonomous aircraft can land in tight spaces between buildings and carry medical equipment and a patient. They don't need a pilot, so paramedics can focus on helping the patient while the aircraft flies itself to the hospital.

20. Some future cars will have holographic displays floating in front of the windshield! Instead of looking down at a screen, you'll see navigation arrows, speed, and warnings floating in the air. The holograms move with your head so they're always easy to see. It's like having magical floating road signs!

21. The Volocopter is like a giant drone you can ride in! This electric aircraft has 18 rotors and can fly itself using computers. It's designed to be an air taxi in cities and can land on special platforms on top of buildings. Imagine taking a flying taxi to avoid traffic jams!

22. Future trucks might drive in "platoons" like a train on the highway! The lead truck is driven by a human, but the trucks behind it follow automatically using special sensors. They can drive very close together to save fuel and take up less space on the road. It's like having a conga line of self-driving trucks!

23. Some concept cars can read your emotions! They use cameras to watch your face and can tell if you're tired, angry, or happy. If you're getting sleepy, the car might make the seats vibrate or change the lighting to help you stay awake. It's like having a car that knows how you're feeling!

24. The Pop.Up Next is a car that can attach to a giant drone! When traffic is bad, a large drone can pick up the passenger cabin and fly it to your destination. The wheels stay behind and drive themselves to a parking spot. It's like having a car that can transform into a flying pod!

25. Future racing cars might not need drivers! Companies are developing autonomous race cars that can drive faster and safer than human drivers. These cars use artificial intelligence to learn the best racing lines and can react faster than any human. Imagine watching a race where robots compete against each other!

26. Some future cars will be made from recycled ocean plastic! Companies are finding ways to turn plastic waste from the ocean into car parts. One concept car's seats are made from recycled fishing nets, and its body panels are made from plastic bottles. Your future car could help clean up the ocean!

27. The Terrafugia Transition can fold its wings in under a minute! This flying car can fit in a normal garage when its wings are folded. It runs on regular car gasoline and can drive on any road when it's not flying. The company is already taking orders – you could own one in the next few years!

28. Future emergency vehicles might hover above traffic! Companies are developing rescue vehicles that can fly over traffic jams using electric rotors. They don't need a runway and can land almost anywhere. Some designs even include a special pod that can detach and fly patients directly to the hospital roof!

29. The Protean 360+ has wheels that can turn all the way around! Each wheel can spin in any direction independently, letting the car move sideways, diagonally, or spin in place like a top. The wheels also have their own electric motors inside them – there's no engine under the hood at all!

30. Some future cars might run on air! Companies are developing cars that use compressed air to power their engines instead of gasoline. The air is stored in special tanks like scuba diving tanks, and you can refill them using an air compressor. These cars release only clean air when they drive – no pollution at all!

31. The Aptera Solar Car looks like something from another planet! This three-wheeled car is covered in solar panels and can drive up to 1,000 miles on a single charge – that's like driving from New York to Florida! It's so aerodynamic that it uses less energy than your home's refrigerator to drive at highway speeds. The car never

needs to be plugged in if you drive less than 40 miles per day!

Printed in Great Britain
by Amazon